D1242164

"I found the book to be insightful and entertaining—a must read for any investor desiring to stay ahead of the curve. Kurt really shed some light on the great possibilities that lie ahead."

—Craig Grabau, Certified Public Accountant, Grabau & Company, P. C.

"Most of us (including myself) are intimidated by the complex world of finance and how best to structure our investments for our retirement and family. In his new book, Kurt explains the basic essentials of what you need to know and makes it easy to see where to go from here to meet your goals. And because he does this with a pervasive sense of optimism and down-home Iowa charm, it is a surprisingly easy and quick read!"

—James Albright, Partner at Wilkinson Barker Knauer, LLP

"Even in a positive-looking future, investors can make mistakes including choice of advisors. This must-read, down-to-earth volume will help you see and sidestep many pitfalls."

—Donald Cassidy, President, Retirement Investing Institute, Retired Senior Analyst, Lipper/Thompson Reuters, Author, *It's When You Sell That Counts*

THE FUTURE IS
Brighter
THAN YOU THINK

Kurt D. Cambier, CFP®, ChFC®

Copyright © 2014 by Kurt Cambier

All rights reserved. No part of this book may be used or reproduced in any manner whatsoever without prior written consent of the publisher except in the case of brief quotations embodied in critical articles and reviews. Special book excerpts or customized printings can be created to fit specific needs.

For more information contact:
Kurt Cambier
866-511-1281

ISBN Hardcover: 978-1-939758-95-8
ISBN eBook: 978-1-939758-96-5

Library of Congress Control Number: 2014916497

DISCLOSURE: Registered Representative, Securities offered through Cambridge Investment Research, Inc., a Broker/Dealer, Member FINRA & SIPC Investment Advisor Representative, Cambridge Investment Research Advisors, Inc., a Registered Investment Advisor. Cambridge and Centennial Capital Partners are not affiliated.

CONTENTS

CONTENTS

CHAPTER ONE

Listening to the Noise

I have some good news for you.

I'm sure that you can probably count on one hand the times you've heard that recently. I'm sure it probably won't even take one hand to count the number of times that you have heard that from someone in the financial industry lately. It's no secret that no matter where you turn, you're mostly hearing a myriad of reasons why the doom and gloom isn't going to clear up any time soon. Hopefully I'll be able to help change all of that today.

As a Certified Financial Planner (CFP®) and Chartered Financial Consultant (ChFC®) with twenty-eight years of experience under my belt, I'm no stranger to delivering complete and accurate reports to my clients, some of whom are among the estimated ten thousand baby boom generation Americans retiring every day. Like you, they've worked hard to build their wealth. Like you, they worry about the future—if they'll be able to realize the dreams they've been saving for, and if they'll be able to leave that wealth to the people they love and trust. And just like you, I've told them time and time again that despite what the naysayers may say, good things are not only possible, but also probable.

A good financial planner should be able to see things before they become clear. I pride myself on standing outside of that herd and being able to give forward-looking advice to my clients so that they, too, can stay ahead of the curve. However, you don't just become forward thinking by accident or by the wave of some magic wand or by trying to pick winning stocks. To truly be forward thinking, you must be able to look back and understand history. Once you understand the history of anything—and this includes the market in all its variety and volatility—you stand a better chance of being successful. You have knowledge. And that knowledge is the ultimate, and perhaps only, power that investors have at their disposal.

I live by the idea that this history is an invaluable tool. I always tell my clients who have recently lost someone they love that one way to ensure the person always lives on in their lives and the lives of their children is to think of one characteristic of that person that he or she admired the most and then emulate that characteristic for the rest of his or her life. My mother was a schoolteacher. The way I keep her alive in me is through my commitment to education and history, and I bring that commitment to the table with my clients. I spend a significant amount of time helping clients better understand what they own and why they own it. Taking time to educate my clients gives them more confidence in their plans and dramatically improves their chances of success.

This is particularly important when one is talking about economic history. As in world history or political history, economic history repeats itself. In the short run, economic cycles are not predictable, but in the long run, they become more clear. Looking at the long view of even the most volatile time periods can reveal patterns.

There is, for example, what I refer to as the Wall Street Waltz. Consider this data provided by JP Morgan Asset Management on the subject.

Bear Market Cycles vs. Subsequent Bull Runs S&P 500

MARKET PEAK	MARKET LOW	BEAR MARKET RETURN	LENGTH OF DECLINE	BULL RUN	LENGTH OF RUN	YRS TO REACH OLD PEAK
05/29/46	05/19/47	-28.6%	12	257.6%	122	3.1
07/15/57	10/22/57	-20.7%	3	88.4%	50	0.9
12/21/61	06/26/62	-28.0%	6	79.8%	44	1.2
02/09/66	10/07/66	-22.2%	8	48.0%	26	0.6
11/29/68	05/26/70	-36.1%	18	72.4%	31	1.8
01/05/73	10/03/74	-48.4%	21	125.6%	74	5.8
11/28/80	08/12/82	-27.1%	20	228.8%	60	0.2
08/25/87	12/04/87	-33.5%	3	582.1%	148	1.6
03/24/00	10/09/02	-49.1%	31	101.5%	60	4.6
10/09/07	03/09/09	-56.8%	17	177.0%	60	—
AVERAGE:		-35.0%	14mos	176.0%	68mos	2.2
Source: JP Morgan Asset Management						

This data reveals that when the markets go up, they go up an average of 176 percent over an average of sixty-eight months. When these same markets go down, they decline an average of 35 percent for fourteen months. Hence, the Wall Street Waltz: the markets go five steps forward and one step back.

An example of this would be someone who will turn sixty-two in 2014. This person would have been born in 1952, when the S&P

500 ended the year at 25. In 2013, it broke above 1,800. During this meteoric rise, we experienced many difficulties: the Korean War, the Vietnam War, the assassination of President Kennedy, the impeachment of President Nixon, the Arab oil embargo, the farm crisis, savings and loan collapses, commercial real estate depression, Y2K, the tech bubble collapse, 9/11, and the most recent housing and credit collapse of 2008. If this investor listened to all of the noise of the crisis du jour, he would have panicked, rushed out of the market, and missed the huge gains present in the S&P 500 index and the market as a whole.

The prevailing hope—and here, again, we are talking about the herd mentality that good investors and advisors try to separate themselves from—is that once the markets are on a progressively upward trend, they'll never step back. History has told us that this obviously isn't the case. The great Wall Street titan Sir John Templeton knew as much when he said, "Bull markets are born on pessimism, grow on skepticism, mature on optimism, and die on euphoria. The time of maximum pessimism is the best time to buy, and the time of maximum optimism is the best time to sell."

This is an exceptionally eloquent version of the common philosophy to buy low and sell high. By understanding history and appreciating trends, one can learn not how to follow, but instead, how to lead. When the euphoria seems to be unchecked—when one "can't possibly lose" by buying real estate or "can't possibly lose" by buying a technology stock—this is the time when the real historians, the true visionaries, understand that a correction is not only inevitable, but near. To see some examples of how the daily noise can mislead you, look at some of these headlines that have popped up throughout the years. A *Time* magazine article on September 9, 1974, titled "Seeking Relief from a Massive Migraine," read like this: "Investors have been frightened of an economy that seems out of control . . . the stock market has scarcely been so shaky since 1929 . . . a Gallup poll published last month found that 46 percent of adults feared a depression similar to the classic one of the 1930s."

On December 3, 1984, an article titled, "Banking Takes a Beating," the statement, "Bankers now face their most strenuous survival test since the Great Depression" appeared in *Time* magazine.

My all-time favorite is the August 13, 1979, article in *Business Week* titled, "The Death of Equities," which reads: "The old attitude of buying solid stocks as a cornerstone for one's life savings and retirement has simply disappeared. The death of equities is a near-permanent condition."

The day that article was published, the Dow Jones closed at 875.26. I want to remind you that we broke through 16,000 on the Dow in 2013. If that's a permanent death, it was followed by quite a resurrection. My point here is bad news sells copy, and what the media gives you is not sound financial information but in most cases is simply financial pornography.

I don't want you to get confused about my point here, thinking that history repeating itself will mean only the bad things will come to pass, cycling through at just the wrong time for you and your investments. On the contrary, my good news for you is that the bad news is temporary, just as it always is. We are living in a wonderful time and in a wonderful country. We are living in a world of unprecedented access to technology, of new developments in health care and globalization, of a shifting of the very fabric of how we communicate with one another.

And the demographics are on our side. The largest generation in the United States is no longer the baby boomers but the baby boomers' babies, also known as Generation Y. Generation Y is made up of the kids born from 1984 to 2002. As the younger generations grow up and move up, as they prepare to earn more and spend more, there will be shifts in the marketplace. Generation Y will provide a similar boost to the economy that the baby boomer generation did.

And let's not forget the emerging world: China, India, Brazil, and others, who will provide huge marketplaces for increased consumption and spending. In the Super-Cycle Report, the groundbreaking report by the Standard Chartered Bank, it's been stated that in the past, most of the world's growth came from 18 percent of the world's population: the United States, Japan, and Europe. In the future, most of the world's growth will come from 85 percent of the world's population: the vast emerging world.

We will experience times of creative destruction. That is when one industry will fail or become outdated as another new, more efficient one blossoms in its place. Some of those shifts will result in inevitable tumult, but some of those shifts will be uplifting. With planning, hard work, preparation, and an appreciation for the groundwork that has been laid for us by history itself, I know that you can capitalize on these trends toward success.

CHAPTER TWO

I Wasn't Born on Third Base, Thinking I Hit a Triple

One of the reasons I'm so intent on keeping history alive—in keeping the stories of my forebears close to my heart—is that my own history has heavily influenced my own trajectory. Without my history, and without my struggles, my success never would have come to pass. And it's not just my history that I work to honor—my family history plays a large part in how I strive to live my life and to bring success to my clients.

When my mother, Virginia Cambier, was only two years old, her mother died of breast cancer. Her father was an illiterate German immigrant who was, in a short time, widowed and left to care for his seven children. He quickly became overwhelmed with the considerable responsibilities left to him. Because he was uneducated, unprepared, and burdened with a lack of understanding of the English language, he had his farm in Minnesota quitclaim deeded away from him by a neighbor. He knew he could no longer sustain the health and welfare of his children, so he drove my mother and her siblings down from Minnesota to my great-grandfather's farm in Remsen, Iowa.

Already in his late sixties, my great-grandfather wasn't necessarily in a better place to care for his late daughter's children. He did what he could, putting all seven in a Catholic orphanage in Sioux City, Iowa, and paid a monthly fee in exchange for the assurance that none of his grandchildren would be adopted out and that way the family would stay together. I remember visiting that orphanage as a child in the late '60s, and I remember how my mother chuckled when she heard that they were closing the orphanage because it was too crowded.

At the time it closed, it only housed sixty-five children. In my mother's day, the Depression era, the orphanage housed around 360 children. My mother told me how the mattresses were scattered all over the gymnasium floor, and everyone slept side by side, with the boys on one side of the gym and the girls on the other. It was standard practice, at that time, to release the boys at age twelve and the girls at age fifteen, when the hormones would begin to rage, so that the orphanage wouldn't have any more children to take care of.

My mother worked it out so that she could be released at age twelve, along with her twin brother, Virgil. They lived in Remsen, Iowa, with their aunt, Clara Gossling, who was a true saint. She never married, and yet cared for all of those children. When my mother was eighteen, she attended Briar Cliff College in Sioux City, Iowa, to begin her education to become a schoolteacher. Soon after, tragedy struck her again. She contracted polio and was told by her doctor that she would never walk again. True to her fighting spirit, she overcame her disease to prove the doctors wrong.

After marrying my father, she had two miscarriages, the last coming after an appendicitis attack when my sister Debbie, who only lived three days, was born prematurely. My mother persisted in making a family, ultimately giving birth to four children. Five years after my mother began her battle with breast cancer, my sister Carla was born. She was only six months old when my mother died. I was ten years old when she passed away. Watching my mother fight and suffer for five years, trying to be with her children, left a profound mark on my life.

My father was a rebel who dropped out of school in the ninth grade and moved away to live on his own at the age of fourteen. He began working for the railroad, then in a packing plant, before becoming a long-haul truck driver, which he did for fifteen years. An eternal entrepreneurial spirit, he put all of his chips on the table and started Cambier Ready Mix in Alton, Iowa, the funds for which he got mostly from my mother's life insurance policy. The ready mix business led to the formation of Midwest Precast, a leading agricultural construction company. In its best year, 1979, he employed one hundred people and grossed $7 million in revenue.

He thought it was never going to end, but it did. When the farm crisis of the 1980s hit, it destroyed my father's fourteen-year-old business. Suddenly he found himself without money, uneducated, and defeated. On December 30, 1984, he suffered a massive heart attack. I remember the day well, because it was my birthday and I had just moved to Colorado. When I received the phone call to tell me they were calling the family in because he wasn't expected to make it, I spent the night tossing and turning, alone in a strange place. That was a long and lonely night.

But just like my mother, my father was a fighter. The doctors told him he needed a heart transplant and would only live six months. He never got the transplant, took twenty-four pills and three shots of insulin daily, had only 25 percent of his heart working, and lived another five years. My father died the same week I met Jeannette, the woman who would become my wife. God truly does work in mysterious but meaningful ways: when I lost one person I loved, he brought a new one into my life.

This leads me to the story of how I got to Colorado, became a CFP® professional, ChFC®, and a partner with Centennial Capital Partners. I had my own life-and-death struggle at the age of twelve. In the summer between seventh and eighth grades, I suffered a ruptured appendix. The organ leaked poison, which then spread throughout my body, leaving me gravely ill. The surgeons told my father that they didn't know if I would make it out of surgery. I spent the next three months of that summer in and out of the hospital, and I went from a strapping 120 pounds down to a frail 80 pounds. When all the other boys were growing, my body was fighting to survive. I entered high school a five-foot-one, 110 pound weakling (quite a contrast to my six-foot-three frame today!), and I was known as Kurt the Squirt.

But ultimately, the groundwork had been laid for my fighting spirit. I left Iowa after my father's business failed and my own attempt at enterprise failed. After I graduated from the University of South Dakota, I borrowed money and invested in a take-and-bake pizza franchise in Spencer, Iowa, known as Pizza Unlimited. I had the fifth-best-performing store out of 68 in the franchise chain. Unfortunately the farm crisis had hit, farms were foreclosed on (more banks failed in the 1980s than in 2008) and I went broke.

I loaded everything I had in my car and drove to Colorado, where I worked a few odd construction jobs before landing in Denver with fourteen dollars in my pocket, no job, and no place to live. The year was 1984, and I was driving a 1964 Plymouth Valiant. I found a place to live, began working as one of those dreaded telemarketers selling Time Life books. It was part-time work that allowed me to earn enough to live on, and yet afforded me the time to find a full-time job.

Eventually I got hired by an insurance company to sell insurance. I knew no one, so I would grab a handful of business cards and go out on Saturday mornings and knock on doors. Eventually one thing led to another. I became a member of the Million Dollar Round Table, then Court of the Table of the Million Dollar Round Table and many presidents' and leaders' clubs along the way. All of that was done without a complaint at any level, and I became a gold-star member of the Better Business Bureau.

Along the way, Jeannette became my wife and gave birth to our three beautiful children: Kameron, Christian, and Carsen. Shortly after Carsen was born, Jeannette became sick. After weeks of tests, doctors narrowed her possible illness down to three things—cancer, lupus, or multiple sclerosis—eventually diagnosing her with MS, the effects of which we live with today. It was scary, having three young children and not knowing the fate of my wife. It gave me a clearer understanding of how my father must have felt when my mother was ill.

With all the things that have happened to me, I still feel very blessed. I have a loving family, great business partners, and a group of clients I truly love and care for. It pains me greatly when I hear of people in my profession who have misled clients, or roped them into elaborate Ponzi schemes, stealing their life savings. I take to heart the words of my father when he spoke of providing a service: "Do what you say you're going to do when you say you're going to do it."

A very wise man, he also once told me, "Son, if you remember that the world owes you nothing, then you will be fine." I have hit a few triples in my day, but I certainly wasn't born on third base.

CHAPTER THREE

A Study of Demographics

Favorite old sayings, while undoubtedly the simplest things you can hear, end up applying to so much of my complicated industry. In fact, these sayings can apply to anyone's industry, or anyone's life, and it's sage advice, so I think one of them bears repeating here: the good Lord gave us two ears and only one mouth—and most of us need to take the hint.

Personally, I've learned a lot from listening to people. I've learned valuable life lessons from my family, watching them move with incredible strength and grace through some really hard circumstances. I've learned equally valuable lessons from my colleagues and clients, who continue to teach me as I move through the school of life. And what's more, we're living in an age of unprecedented freedom of information, which means great things for someone like me—and hopefully, someone like you—as I am constantly trying to learn and improve my business practices based on honoring the lessons and values of history. Put simply, there's a lot out there to listen to, which is precisely how I came to arrive at a central theory of my practice, one that combines historical research on economics, markets, and demographics.

One of the great sources of information I have found concerning the world's demographics and the possible effect those demographics may have on the economy came from the Standard Chartered Bank of England's Super-Cycle Report. The Standard Chartered Bank is one of the largest and oldest banks in the developed world. Three-fourths of the Standard Bank's business is in countries throughout Asia and Africa—a good portion of the developing world—and so they have a wonderful perspective about what the global economy will truly look like, as opposed to just a cross section of the American economy. As we go through this chapter, I'll be referring to these figures:

Super-Cycle Report

	1990	USD trn	2000	USD trn	2010	USD trn	2020	USD trn	2030	USD trn
1	US	5.8	US	10	US	14.6	China	24.6	China	73.5
2	Japan	3	Japan	4.7	China	5.9	US	23.3	US	38.2
3	Germany	1.5	Germany	1.9	Japan	0.6	India	9.6	India	30.3
4	France	1.2	UK	1.5	Germany	3.3	Japan	6	Brazil	12.2
5	Italy	1.1	France	1.3	France	2.6	Brazil	5.1	Indonesia	9.3
6	UK	1	China	1.2	UK	2.3	Germany	5	Japan	8.4
7	Canada	0.6	Italy	1.1	Italy	2	France	3.9	Germany	8.2
8	Spain	0.5	Canada	0.7	Brazil	2	Russia	3.5	Mexico	6.6
9	Brazil	0.5	Brazil	0.6	Canada	1.6	UK	3.4	France	6.4
10	China	0.4	Mexico	0.6	Russia	1.5	Indonesia	3.2	UK	5.6
Source: IMF, Standard Chartered Research										

From the data in the Super-Cycle Report over the past century, you can see that about two-thirds of the world's economic growth has come from 18 percent of the world's population: Europe, Japan, and the United States—or the initial industrialized world. This isn't going to be true in the future; over the next twenty years, the Super-Cycle Report estimates that two-thirds of the world's economic growth will come from the emerging world: countries like China, India, Brazil, Indonesia, and Mexico.

This is where the optimism comes in. If we follow the Super-Cycle Report to the conclusions it predicts, we're not going to see decline in growth from the industrialized world—that will still be there, despite everyone's concerns about the continued ripple effect (and sometimes, quite frankly, tsunami effect) from the recession of 2008. My optimism comes from the fact that these emerging middle-class populations around the world are going to make better lives for us all as they better their own.

Capitalism does amazing things for the world's poor, ultimately taking them out of poverty and making them earners and consumers in the middle class. When we look at the billions of people in the emerging world and what they represent, it's hard *not* to be optimistic, I'd argue. Consumption and the velocity with which money moves drive economies.

BE HAPPY: WE'RE IN A SUPERCYCLE

A supercycle, as you may be able to guess from looking at these reports, is when the whole world prospers. And right now, despite all of the fear and worry present in the media, we're in a supercycle.

The Super-Cycle Report breaks down the other supercycles we've experienced globally. By matching up the dates to the historical events occurring at the time, you can better understand—and hence, to some extent, predict—when other supercycles will occur.

One of the first supercycles began in the late 1880s and lasted until 1914. This time was essentially the industrial revolution; at the beginning of the cycle, the United States wasn't considered a world power, but by the end, it had risen to number one. At the end of this supercycle, the world gross domestic product (GDP) growth had doubled, from a stagnant 1 percent to 2 percent. That had a remarkable effect on the entire world.

From 1915 to 1946, however, there was no supercycle. This was the era of World Wars I and II and the Great Depression. But after World War II, when Japan and Europe were rebuilt, and the United States wasn't using its industrial might for warfare, but rather was building automobiles and washing machines, world GDP growth jumped to 5 percent, a stream of growth that lasted from 1946 to 1973—the greatest supercycle we've experienced to date.

This was followed up by an era of stagflation—a flat period—that began with the Arab oil embargoes of the 1970s. This flat period lasted all the way up to the year 2000. While many investors in the United States tended to see the bull markets of the 1980s and '90s as supercycle-like in the prosperity it created in our country, this wasn't a supercycle according to the definition set forth by the Standard Chartered Bank studies. When the United States prospered during that time period, the S&P 500 was growing in the double digits. This was a time that most Americans thought would last forever. Meanwhile, the international markets had below-average returns, in the low single digits. Remember, the true definition of a supercycle is when the entire world experiences above average growth.

So that brings us to now, and it brings us to why I continue to be so optimistic. The next supercycle is, in fact, happening now. The big population centers of the world, like China and India, have started to promote access to education. The literacy levels in those countries have skyrocketed, even surpassed the United States in some places. When literacy levels rise, the newly literate move from low-paying, rural jobs to urban centers, where they earn more and consume more. The beauty of capitalism begins to work its magic, and prosperity gives power (and purchasing power) to people who had none before. As this purchasing power grows, so do economies.

Because of the way the global economy is intertwined right now, this growth means big things for the already-developed world, too. As these countries do well, so will we. Big multinational US corporations will continue to grow. The American technology and ingenuity that serves (and is served by) those countries will grow as well. As other standards of living increase, so will ours.

POPULATION GROWTH AND THE SUPERCYCLE

Because of an aging population and lack of young people, Europe and Japan's future growth will remain flat. In the emerging world, however, particularly in China, the population is very young. The average age of a person in China at the time of this writing is believed to be around nineteen. This is huge; they haven't even reached their peak period of earning and spending yet.

I once heard a speech given by Mark Zinder, the former vice president of communications at Franklin Templeton Funds. He broke down the population of the United States into four age groups: learners (birth to 25), yearners (25 to 35), earners (35 to 65), and burners (65 and older). When the yearners transition to earners, they'll eventually be spearheading and generating much of the economic growth in the United States. Americans hit their peak earning years starting at age 35 and really ramp up their earning, spending, and investing by age 50, and this continues to age 65.

Speaking of listening and learning from the lessons of history, this is very much what happens with each of these demographics—and that's why understanding the context of each of these demographic groups' decisions is key to understanding the optimism that I have for our global economic future. Each of these segments of the population is heavily influenced by what they witnessed during their learning and yearning stages, before they became earners. It shaped who they are and how they earn and spend, how they live their lives. Just as the events of my parents' and grandparents' lives shaped me growing up, so do the events of these generations' parents' and grandparents' lives—as well as historical events on a global scale.

Take, for example, the seventy-eight million baby boomers who were born from 1946 to 1964. They were greatly impacted by what their parents' generation went through. Known as the Greatest Generation, the parents of the boomers were born from 1927 to 1945. They experienced the Great Depression and fought in World War II. Because of the extreme hardship endured by their parents, the baby boomers were a bit slow to become spenders. They began really impacting the economy when they entered their peak earning years. The earning years, by Zinder's definition, are from thirty-five to age sixty-five. If you take the beginning of this generation of baby boomers beginning in 1946 and add thirty-five years to that year you get 1981, which was the beginning of the great US bull market that began in the '80s and lasted until the year 2000. Much of this is owed to the baby boomer generation's consumption and investing.

When we look at the second baby boom—the eighty million people in Generation Y, born from 1984 to 2002—it looks a bit different. Just as the Great Depression influenced the baby boomers, the recessions of the 2000s have haunted the Y generation. Because their parents suffered through the tech bubble, the credit collapse, and the corresponding real estate collapse, they are disillusioned with that sort of aspirational property ownership. They want to rent or buy a loft rather than buy a big house. They are urbanites, where their parents were suburbanites.

But where the baby boomers reacted to the Depression by scrimping and saving, Generation Y has reacted by pulling away from saving, after seeing their parents become disenchanted with the dwindling returns from their 401(k)s and pensions. Instead, they're actively spending during their yearning years, buying new technology and replacing it frequently. The upside to all of this is that they're hitting their spending peak earlier—no doubt contributing to the kickoff of the bull market that began in 2009, which is what some experts say is to be the biggest bull market we'll see in our lifetimes. As Mark Zinder put it, we're about to do it all over again.

The wild card in all of this, of course, is the emerging world, those densely populated, rapidly literate countries like China and India. There's no reason to assume that the growth happening in those countries isn't going to continue. While recessions will happen, and markets will fall, the smart investor will listen to and learn from history's lessons and get on the bus, so to speak, by investing in the great companies of the world—otherwise, that investor risks getting left in the dust.

That is one of the reasons why it's so important to have a financial strategy that includes investments that will help you stay ahead of the rising costs and any other inflationary pressures we will see. As we know from history, inflation happens not only when prices increase, but also when wages increase. It's actually *deflationary* if fixed costs for the consumer—like food and energy—go up while wages stay flat. More money has to be spent on the staples of life and less on new cars and electronics.

But if wages increase, then the consumer has more money to continue to spend on these items, and that's when inflation happens. The classic definition of inflation, as given by famed University of Chicago economics professor Milton Friedman, is "too much money chasing too few goods and services." If you're not invested in something that will help you keep up with or surpass inflationary patterns, you're going to be behind the eight ball.

CHAPTER FOUR

Recessions Will Happen

I've talked a little bit already about the Wall Street Waltz—the inevitable volatility of the markets. Since World War II, the S&P 500 has gone up an average of 176 percent for sixty-eight months, only to fall an average of 35 percent for fourteen months. Hence, the waltz: five steps forward, one step back. During that time, the longest and largest upside, the great bull market beginning in the 1980s, lasted for 148 months, gaining 582 percent. The longest decline in that period might sting a little more, for it happened more recently: the market went down over 56 percent in a period lasting for seventeen months, bottoming out in March of 2009.

So if the waltz is so inevitable, why does it still hurt so much? It's because most investors never expect it to happen. It really comes down to a lack of knowledge of market cycles. Even the most savvy businessperson can't help but get wrapped up in the emotional roller coaster of the economy. When things are going well, it doesn't seem like things will ever go poorly again. But I'm here to tell you that they will. This doesn't contradict the optimism I've expressed in earlier chapters, but it's a reality that lives alongside that optimism. A good financial advisor will *always* tell you that recessions are going to happen, just as he or she will be honest with you that there's no way for your financial plan to completely bypass these bumpy periods. What makes that financial advisor a good one, other than honesty, is that he or she will help you develop not only a strategy for bull markets, but a solid strategy for bear markets as well, helping you lessen the emotional surprises that come with them.

WHAT CAUSES RECESSIONS, AND WHY CAN'T WE STOP THEM?

Just as no one factor solely causes an up-trending market, no one factor causes market downturns. Geopolitical issues, deflation, inflation, and falling corporate profits are all common culprits in these modern times. Market declines have been commonplace from 1900–2012, as markets have experienced a 5 percent correction on average of three times per year, a 10 percent correction once a year, a 15 percent correction every two years, and a 20 percent correction every three years. A person turning sixty-two today will have seen numerous corrections, nine full-blown recessions, and scores of panicked investors' reactions during those periods.

Remember that someone turning sixty-two in 2014 would have been born in 1952, when the S&P 500 closed at 25. It eventually broke through 1,800 in 2013, giving substance to the phrase, "Market advances are permanent, market declines are temporary." As pointed out in the previous chapter on demographics, this undoubtedly had some influence on that individual investor's outlook. In fact, it's the panic caused by individual investors that largely make these periods of correction and recession much worse than they ultimately need to be.

The irrational behavior of individual investors is precisely why a good financial advisor is necessary to temper the enthusiasm—and panic—that can occur during periods of market upturn and downturn. The market's performance and an individual investor's performance are not necessarily one in the same. Consider the following information from Dalbar Inc., a leading market research firm:

Emotional Impact on Clients Equity Market Return
vs.
Equity Mutual Fund Investor Returns* (1988–2008)

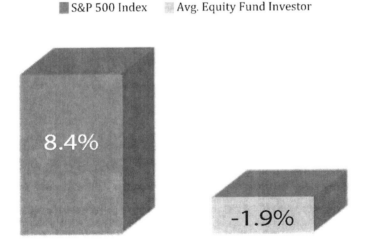

■ S&P 500 Index ▨ Avg. Equity Fund Investor

8.4%

-1.9%

*SOURCE: Dalbar, Inc. Quantitative Analysis of Investor Behavior—2008. Represents average annually compounded returns of equity indices vs. equity mutual fund investors; based on the length of time shareholders actually remain invested in a fund and the historic performance of the funds appropriate index. Past performance is no guarantee of future results. Investors cannot invest directly in an index.

What I like most about this information is that it shows the near bottom of the market—the last great recession we experienced as a society, in 2008. As compared to times of relative market prosperity, this period shows some tough numbers: the S&P 500 index averaged only an 8.4 percent return. Still a positive return, nonetheless, but nothing like the chart-topping returns that we've seen in the past. The individual investor's performance, however, is even lower: it's in the *negatives,* at -1.9 percent. What the research shows is that over an extended period of time the individual investor not only underperforms the market but underperforms the investments they invest in. The culprit is irrational behavior. The number-one cause of investment failure is the investor himself.

Individual investors definitely recognize that they can perform well when the market performs well, and when the market performs poorly, they're likely to see portfolio declines. But I bet that if you polled a group of seasoned individual investors on this particular issue, they'd be a little surprised. How could their performance be so far off from the market?

Much like the factors that cause the recessions themselves, there are a variety of answers to this question, and some of the pitfalls are more common than others. Trying to time the market is one common possibility—history has shown us that individual investors who attempt to guess when the market is about to take an upturn (or a nosedive) are almost always wrong, and mutual fund inflows and outflows are the best evidence of this. At market peaks, the inflows into equity mutual funds reach a peak, and in market bottoms, outflows soar.

A savvy investor would do just the opposite. Poor behavior on the part of the individual investor is nearly always to blame for dramatically underperforming the market. And *all* individual investors, no matter how smart or accomplished in their professional field, fall victim to this to some degree, so much so that the giants of the financial industry have some oft-quoted wisdom that applies to just this situation.

Take Warren Buffett, one of the most successful investors of our time, who famously lives by the maxim: "I get nervous when others get greedy, and greedy when others get nervous." To say that he knows what he's talking about is an understatement: with a net worth of about $60 billion according to *Forbes*, he walks the walk as much as he talks the talk.

Famed former Fidelity fund manager Peter Lynch also put his two cents in when he said, "Far more money has been lost by investors preparing for corrections or trying to anticipate corrections than have been lost by the corrections themselves." And it was Wharton School of Business economics professor Jeremy Siegel, in his book *Stocks for the Long Run,* who correctly pointed out that "fear plays a bigger role in human behavior than does the impressive weight of historical evidence."

The lesson in all of this is that we can't stop the corrections; they've come and gone, just as they will continue to come and go over the years. But what a good financial advisor will do is to develop a plan of action anticipating that these events *will* occur, and instead of trying to avoid them, will try to capitalize on them.

MAKING A GOOD DEFENSE
PART OF YOUR OFFENSE

The best way to prepare for these inevitable recessions and corrections is to go into the process with your eyes wide-open. Understand that recessions and corrections will happen, and make a plan for them. When establishing a portfolio, a downside bias should be discussed—in other words, what type of risk or decline can the client or investor truly tolerate before they start losing sleep? I like to call this the Sominex effect: a client should always be able to go to sleep at night after the decisions that they've made. If the decisions are keeping them up, then it's time to make some different decisions or take the time to learn more. Remember, knowledge is power, so be informed.

You'll notice that I'm speaking about this in terms of portfolio *declines* rather than *losses*. This distinction is an important one, and it goes back to making smart decisions as a reasoned, reasonable investor rather than knee-jerk decisions based on emotions. Simply put, a market decline or portfolio decline is not a loss unless you sell into that decline, making it a loss. If you get nervous and pull your money out of the market and back into cash, then you've certainly taken that loss. But if you hold the course—provided it was a reasonable, reasoned, and, of course, researched course to begin with—that money will be able to bounce back when the market bounces back. It has retained its elasticity, and in some cases will even better position you for the future as compared to peers who have decided to wait until the market has recovered and moved higher again to buy in.

A great example of this is how Nick Murray's book *Simple Wealth, Inevitable Wealth* describes Warren Buffett. On the day of the great crash of October 19, 1987, his company Berkshire Hathaway closed at $3,170 a share. This represented a decline in value that day to Buffett of $6.2 billion. Notice I said it was a *decline*, not a *loss.* Why was it not a loss? Because Buffett didn't sell. Recently, Berkshire Hathaway stock closed at over $160,000 a share.

If you'll recall, Buffett famously said he gets nervous when others get greedy, and he gets greedy when others get nervous. He used the 2008 crisis to buy big positions in iconic names like GE and Goldman Sachs, as well as purchasing two railroads. I always tell my clients if you sell your stocks in a panic, you are selling them to the richest people in the world, and you're helping them become richer.

Another common pitfall of the individual investor is failing to understand the power of dollar cost averaging. As an investor is in accumulation mode during his career, he is often funding his 401(k) or other outside retirement investments for future use. A smart investor—or maybe it's more accurate to say a well-informed investor—will continue to invest the same amount (or even a larger amount) in these retirement vehicles as the market is declining. A reactionary investor will pull his investments back during periods of decline, and wait until the market is on the uptick before investing again. This is another form of buying high and selling low, and it's absolutely detrimental in the long term.

If, for example, this investor is putting $1,000 per month into his 401(k) and the market share price is averaging $20 a share, he is buying fifty shares per month. If, however, the market declines— and over the course of this working person's life, it obviously will— and he invests the same amount of money each month, and the share price falls to $10, he's buying one hundred shares. He is able to purchase more shares while the market is essentially on sale. And while he can't accurately predict the value of the market at any given time, he can control how much of the market shares he owns. In times of decline, by buying a bigger share of the market, it ultimately becomes an opportunity to make a lot more money over the long term.

And these fluctuations will happen; you can count on that, just as surely as you can count on the sun rising tomorrow morning. Having a plan and understanding the risk that you're taking on in your portfolio is the most important thing, and that's something that a good financial advisor can help you with. There are ways to measure risk inside a portfolio that the individual investor doesn't generally have much knowledge about. If a portfolio is broad and balanced, there are ways to mitigate these risks, although it's impossible to completely eliminate them.

Exposing oneself to too much of one segment of the market is also a common error. The tech bubble bursting in 2000 is one recent, memorable example of this. As investors saw double-digit returns every year, they turned a blind eye to how much risk they were taking, seeing only the rewards. The real estate crash was another example of investors taking an unacceptable amount of the same type of risk, thinking that real estate would never go down. Mark Twain told us, "History repeats itself until it doesn't." Boy, was he ever right. However, if you understand the risk you're taking, you won't be surprised by what's in your portfolio. When the risk is known, what lies beyond the equal sign of any equation—the results—are more predictable.

Time horizon coupled with current market conditions are two other factors investors fail to connect. I am not a fan of target date funds—funds that have a year of retirement behind them, say,

Target 2020, for instance. The danger in these funds is that they only look at time horizons and not market conditions. As you approach the target date, they add in more investments, such as bonds, which, depending on market conditions and valuations, may actually pose a higher risk than stocks. My advice is to never use these target date funds.

I view risk management and well-researched asset allocation as being very similar to cooking. I like to cook—mainly, I'll be the first to admit, because I like to eat. Like many of the lessons I learned in life, cooking skills were forced upon me out of necessity—after my mother died, and my sisters could only make a few dishes, mainly macaroni and cheese, and tuna and noodles. A young, growing boy can only eat so much of that. So I picked up the spoons and the pots and I got to it.

What I learned about cooking was a lot like what I've learned about investing, and that's that ingredients are not necessarily the most important thing. Sure, it helps to have fresh, high-quality ingredients when you're trying to create something tasty and healthy. But no matter how good your ingredients are, no matter how locally sourced or organic, you can still be left with a disaster boiling over on your stove if you don't follow the recipe. If your soup has too much of that excellent garlic, that heirloom cilantro, it's going to taste bad.

Having a solid recipe is about finding that balance of garlic to cilantro to broth and so on. Just as in investing, really understanding the allocation and volatility of your investments as a whole—no matter what ingredients those individual investments represent—is what's going to make the biggest impact on your long-term success. It's what's in the soup as a whole, rather than the individual ingredients, that will stand the test of time; what's hot today isn't necessarily going to be hot tomorrow. It's the recipe, or the allocation, of your investments that matter the most. That goes as much for a tech stock as it does a trans fat.

There are times during market cycles when some parts of the economy will be destroyed—along with the jobs that made those pieces run—while others will be created and move into their place. This process—which I briefly discussed in the first chapter, known as creative destruction—is part of what makes the market so change-able, so organic. Throughout time, we've seen some clear examples of how this evolution of markets has shaped the world, largely for the better: the horse and buggy gave way to the train, the automobile, and eventually the airplane. More recently, voice mail has replaced answering services and phone centers, allowing businesses to operate with less overhead and from farther away. E-mails and scans have replaced faxes and letter writing. Cell phones have replaced landlines, and Google has replaced the need for phone books. All of these examples, while they've caused some upheaval at their inception, were inevitable, normal, and largely healthy for the overall economy.

As I often tell people, knowledge is power. Be informed. One great resource is a half-hour-long presentation available on YouTube given by Ray Dalio of Bridgewater Associates, one of the largest hedge funds in the world. Titled "How the Economic Machine Works," this engaging clip does a brilliant job of explaining how these economic shifts and individual investor behavior intertwine to make the cogs turn and the spark plugs ignite inside the rum-bling inner workings of our economy.

Dalio explains that money and credit are essentially the same thing, and that when credit and money are available, people tend to spend them helping economies flourish. When people spend money, it creates jobs, giving other people money and credit to spend. When people *don't* spend money, economies contract, as they tend to do during recessions that are punctuated with panic and belt-tightening. Those jobs go away, and then we slip into economic decline.

Dalio's point is the same as mine—and Buffett's, and Siegel's, and Lynch's—these ups and downs are inevitable, and understanding them, on the whole, might make them less painful to the individual. The problem, of course, is that human nature is to fear what it doesn't understand—and investors are only human, after all. Educating yourself, gaining knowledge and ultimately gaining power, is essential to weathering these economic storms. And there will be storms.

So my question for you is this: How prepared are you?

CHAPTER FIVE

Common Mistakes of the High Net Worth Investor

As much as we'd all like to hope we are truly unique, the reality is that we all have more in common than we think. Living out in Colorado, I'm not immune to it—along with the beautiful vistas, I've subscribed to that rugged individual mentality, the notion that I'm carving my own way. But I'm only human, just like you. There are entire fields—psychology, sociology, and anthropology, to name a few—dedicated to uncovering these commonalities and laying them bare for all to see.

The behavior of investors, even high net worth investors, is no exception. I've talked about erratic investor behavior in previous chapters, and how emotions can throw everything off once they've been put in the mix. Rather than the markets or the economy being the biggest obstacle to investor success, it's irrational decision making on the part of investors themselves that causes underperforming portfolios and exacerbates downturns. It's my hope that by outlining some of the most common investor mistakes for you, you'll be able to avoid some of this all-too-human herd mentality.

NEVER EXPECTING THE UNEXPECTED

Many investors get overconfident when it comes to perceiving their ability to handle their own investments. This is particularly true as technology changes and more discount financial services and firms make themselves available to the typical investor. Even in the heyday of the 1990s, for example, it seemed as though everyone was an investment guru. Tech stocks were booming, credit and assets were flowing, and the mad money mentality made it so that everyone who had a portfolio thought they knew what they were doing. Stock tips get traded in locker rooms and clubhouses, on the golf course and at the water cooler—everyone thinks they understand what the next hot product will be and the right time to get in on it.

In fact, it's usually in times of booming investment markets that I seem to come across these kinds of situations most frequently. As I travel the country meeting with clients and would-be clients who have been referred to me, it seems that in times when the markets are up significantly, investors are reticent to sign on with a financial professional. They see their returns increasing like gangbusters, and money seems to be flying around readily, so why would they want the advice of a professional when they can do it themselves? Or, in the event that they aren't directly making their own decisions, it seems that they have a brother or sister or uncle who is "very good at reading the markets," and they feel safe enough leaving their assets in the hands of that trusted person.

Because I am and always will be a curious person, I then ask these would-be clients what it is that their brother or sister or uncle does for a living. Are they in the financial industry? No. They might be a rancher, a plumber, or in real estate. I'm here to tell you that in times of great market advances, it can look like a rancher, a plumber, or a real estate agent has struck proverbial gold—he or she may get lucky, and your portfolio may do well.

But what's happening in those cases has nothing to do with calculations, nothing to do with market research, nothing to do with the tools that financial professionals have at their disposal to properly look at the portfolio as a whole and understand the risk-to-reward ratio, your time horizon, your risk tolerance, and so on. What's happening is that these portfolios are likely taking on significantly more risk than the market as a whole, and when the market corrects—as it inevitably will—the values of these portfolios will ultimately get crushed.

I've never been a gambler, but my father liked to gamble. When he'd come back from Las Vegas, I'd hear about the times that he won big—when he took home that ten or fifteen or twenty thousand. But it always struck me how I never heard about all the times he *lost* big.

The stock market, particularly in ultrasuccessful boom and bubble times, is a lot like this kind of gambling. You hear about the successes and you get greedy, thinking it'll be easy to have your own. But the true success is being able to win when everybody else is losing—or losing less than everybody else, as in the recession of 2008.

Today, with the speed of information and the interconnected geopolitical atmosphere that links the world's economies, it's critical that portfolios are structured to limit risk during times of down markets. This doesn't mean that, as an investor, you cash out and lose confidence and reinvest when the market is going up. I've already talked about that detrimental phenomenon, known as buying high and selling low. But what this means is that when the market is turbulent, and it will be, you are able to remain stable and flexible in your investment choices, and adjust your portfolio accordingly. This is something done by the sophisticated financial professional, and not that brother, sister, or uncle who is "good at picking stocks."

One thing I can promise you is that investing is never going to be easy, and it's never going to be a smooth ride. Failing to expect the unexpected is one surefire way to come home with big losses.

TRYING TO TIME THE MARKET

Similar to being overconfident in one's winner-picking abilities is trying to time the market. Knowing that markets rally or decline, it's often tempting during those times to try to predict when the market has hit its peak to sell or when it's bottomed out to buy. But this is nothing more than guesswork, and the problem is that investors usually guess incorrectly. The other problem is that when investors sell and go to cash, in order to make money going back in to the market, they have to be right *twice*, selling at the right time and then buying back in at the right time, which is harder than guessing right the first time.

This is very difficult to do consistently, if at all. One clear example was during the years between 1986 and 2005. The S&P 500 returned an average net of 11.9 percent. During that time, the markets weathered many busts and booms—the tech bubble, the savings and loan failures, the farm crisis, and so on. Over that time period, $10,000 invested in 1986 would have grown to approximately $94,000 in 2005. But according to Dalbar, a well-known research firm that studies and reports on market trends, the average return for an individual investor was only 3.9 percent annually, meaning that same amount of money only grew to $21,000. When you factor in inflation, this *real return* (as opposed to a *stated* return) is not much of a gain.

One of my favorite quotes on this subject comes from the legendary economist John Kenneth Galbraith, who said, "The purpose of market forecasting is to give astrology credibility." He couldn't be more right, and you shouldn't have to look any farther than those aforementioned figures to understand why. Ultimately, it's truly not *timing of* the market, but *time in* the market that really matters.

TAKING TOO MUCH RISK, OR NOT KNOWING
HOW MUCH RISK YOU'RE REALLY TAKING

During times of market booms, people seem to cross the line from being an investor to being a speculator. While the herd mentality might have you think that these are one and the same, or that they're equally valuable strategywise, this couldn't be farther from the truth. Investment is about strategy, and speculation is just that—pure conjecture. An investor buys assets that are priced at a great value, and is diversified, with a well-balanced portfolio that can protect them from the downside and capitalize on the upside.

A speculator chases trends, buying the hot stocks and funds of the day, acting on those water cooler and golf course rumors. A great example of this, again, is the tech boom, when speculators poured most of the money into the tech sector at the high point of the market, just before the major correction took place and the bubble burst. It wasn't as though these buyers were behaving as investors, getting in on the ground floor in a rational manner. They chased the hot stocks, ignoring the more high-quality value stocks that actually fared well after the collapse in 2000.

The problem is, of course, people don't know when they've stopped being an investor and have stepped into speculation until it's too late, until that bubble bursts, until the portfolio sinks and all is lost. These speculators are overconcentrated in one sector as they chase returns in that sector and that sector alone, blindly moving forward on nothing more than rumors and wishes.

TAKING TOO LITTLE RISK OR BEING TOO CONSERVATIVE

I've spoken a lot about human nature. This is in part because it's easy to understand, but it's also in part because I truly believe it's what drives us in business, even in investing, where cooler heads should theoretically prevail. And it's human nature to be afraid of things we don't understand: other cultures, new products, new people, etc. Not understanding the financial world in general, or investing in particular, or even more specifically, the risk involved in investing, is another surefire recipe for fear. While being too aggressive is risky, being too conservative is equally risky: there's a chance, particularly as we're living longer nowadays, that you'll outlive your money. This is not a position I'd want to be in, no more than I would want to be in the position of losing all of my hard-earned money on a hot stock pick that went belly-up.

Let's think about that fictional investor who was born in 1952. Today, in 2014, he would just be turning sixty-two. Let's compare his parents' household expenses when he was born to his expenses last year.

Then vs. Now
Cost of Living Comparisons

	1952	2013
Gallon of Milk	$0.96	$3.46
Loaf of Bread	$0.16	$1.41
New Auto	$1,850	$26,600
Gallon of Gas	$0.20	$3.39
New Home	$16,800	$178,600
Average Income	$3,515	$39,440
Dow Jones	291.90	13,248.44

As you can see, the costs of goods and services increases as time goes on, and the value of the dollar essentially changes. If you're too conservative, your money simply won't keep pace with the purchasing power needed to maintain your lifestyle. Postage stamps are perhaps the clearest example of this: thirty years ago, a first-class stamp cost fifteen cents. As of this writing, they've just approached forty-nine cents, and will likely continue to climb.

This investor's expenses might have at one point been something like $6,000 per month. In a twenty- to thirty-year period, those same expenses may climb to $18,000 per month just to keep pace with climbing inflation and increases in the cost of your standard of living. The increase in costs to maintain your standard of living doesn't care whether or not you've got more mouths to feed, or you're retired and are no longer bringing in the same income.

Investments like cash, CDs, and government treasuries—all conservative investment vehicles—have a very hard time keeping up with inflation. This means that if this investor—or you—is too conservative, his quality of life will decline over time in the golden years rather than keeping up with inflation. This is a process I call going broke safely. To combat this, it's essential that an investor have exposure to higher-risk assets, but in a balanced and calculated manner.

Remember, risk can be measured—and most investors don't have a clue how much risk they are, or are not, taking.

INVESTOR BEHAVIOR

The biggest mistake, although it's wrapped into all the others listed in this chapter, is that investors tend to get too emotional about their own investments. Remember what Siegel said about fear and emotions trumping the "impressive weight of historical evidence"? You can bet that I do, and I take care to caution my clients about it frequently.

The impact of the markets on the delicate psyche of the investor can't be overstated. There's a certain amount of trauma involved in losses, and paradoxically, a certain blind spot involved in those same losses as well. Fear and emotions can make an investor cautious when he should be optimistic. He'll sit on cash, because the last time he put his money into the market on pure speculation, he got burned. He watches the market go up year after year until he can't take it anymore, and he jumps back in when he finally regains his confidence—which is usually when the market has hit its peak and when investments are overvalued. When those investments decline upon correction, the emotional investor sells upon the decline.

One thing that a good financial advisor can and should be able to do for you is to save you from yourself. If you have a clearly thought out, well-researched financial plan in place, a skilled advisor can prevent most of the emotional nonsense that thwarts investors of all kinds every hour of every day.

OVERDIVERSIFICATION

Many times, an investor will hear the advice to diversify and take it to an extreme. He will think that having eggs in more baskets makes him better off than someone who holds them all in one basket. That's true in a sense, but it's also true that you can be *too* spread out, and you can be spread out poorly.

As I said earlier in regard to my cooking experience, there's something to be admired about a certain amount of restraint—and that all-important balance. You have to strike the right balance or allocation of stocks, bonds, and real estate—there has to be a purpose to your plan. You need your plan to fit your specific needs in regard to your risk tolerance. You are no more likely to become a successful investor by picking investments at random as you are to become a four-star chef by throwing random ingredients into the pot. A good allocation is like a good recipe, and your starting plan and your ability to stick to that plan will determine how successful you're going to become.

But there must be a rhyme, and there must be a reason. With each piece of your portfolio, you must know why you own it, when the right time to move away from it will be, when the right time to hold onto it will be, and so on. A financial advisor is absolutely essential in helping to provide this education on allocation.

FAILING TO THINK ABOUT THE EFFECTS OF TAXES ON YOUR WEALTH

If you think investing is a complicated world—and it is—you haven't even begun to understand the meaning of the word *complicated* until you start incorporating the tax code into your financial plan. And many investors fail to do just that. They fail to have the right tax asset location—meaning that they have the wrong assets placed in the wrong structure when it comes to keeping what they have and protecting their wealth from the tax man.

There are three main pieces of the tax code as it relates to investing. The first is that there's an important difference between ordinary income, capital gains, and dividend income. Depending upon your income and your tax bracket, these three items all have an impact on how much wealth you can keep. Capital gains, for example, are usually taxed in a smaller bracket than ordinary income. Dividend income can offer some unique tax advantages as well.

The mistake made here is all too often, growth assets like stocks are held in an IRA, where they lose their favorable capital gains and dividend income treatment. IRAs are usually taxed at a much higher ordinary income rate upon withdrawal. What I tell clients is to hold assets like stocks and real estate in nonqualified accounts to take advantage of more favorable tax treatment, and hold income assets in an IRA. Smart tax planning can make a huge difference in the long run.

The second area encompasses retirement plans, such as IRAs, Roth IRAs, and 401(k)s. Traditional IRAs and 401(k)s are tax deductible when funded but taxed heavily when withdrawn. Roth IRAs and Roth 401(k) deposits are not deductible when funded but the entire amount, growth and all, can be tax-free when withdrawn. Future tax rates and their impact on your money should be considered. The future tax-free Roths seem attractive to me. Many times, investors fail to take advantage of the tax-advantaged retirement accounts that are available to them, and this results in significant losses in the end.

The third area, and the most labyrinthine in some cases, is the estate tax code. Like the other two points we've considered here, this is something that should be undertaken as part of the financial planning process very early on, and should always be done with a qualified Certified Financial Planner (CFP®) or Certified Public Accountant (CPA), and definitely with a qualified estate planning attorney, as part of your planning team. In the next chapter, we'll unpack this issue a little more—as well as how to make sure that you can keep what you've worked so hard to earn.

CHAPTER SIX

Keeping What You Have

As we've discussed in previous chapters, there are many factors that can cause the decline of an investor's portfolio over his lifetime. But even when compared to the sticky issues like geopolitical unrest, the availability of credit, and irrational investor behavior, the biggest threat to an investor's portfolio is future taxation.

This is a situation that has always been and remains a major point for debate across party lines. But the completely objective, bipartisan truth is that when one looks at the true size of the government debt and unfunded liabilities—which are currently estimated to be around $200 *trillion*—one should absolutely be alarmed, no matter which side of the aisle one walks. In an economy that only generated $15 trillion of gross domestic product (GDP) in 2013, someone is going to have to be on the hook to pay the tab.

The government can't make up that kind of shortfall by taxing the have-nots. They're going to have to look to the haves to make a difference. And the chances are, if you're reading this book, you're probably a have. The growing separation between the haves and the have-nots should be concerning. When the top 5 percent of

American wage earners, the haves, don't have the voting influence they use to have, it will be much easier for the government to put taxing pressure on this group. You've worked hard to get to where you are—you've poured your life into your business, your investments, and making a name for yourself. And it's important that if you want to avoid picking up the tab, you work equally hard to keep what you have.

If you're not fully convinced of the scale of the crisis, think about this example from history—which you should know by now is one of my big predictors for what I think is coming up next. The last time our debt-to-GDP ratio approached 120 percent was the aftermath of World War II. During this time, the top tax rate hit 94 percent, and stayed at about 70 percent until 1982. That's a long time to get taxed at the top rate.

In fact, a *Newsweek* article from April 15, 2010, titled "Today Is the Best Tax Day of Your Life," references a Tax Policy Center study that estimates that at current debt and spending levels, the government would have to raise taxes—from 2010 levels—the lowest bracket going from 10 percent to 15 percent and the highest bracket from 35 percent to 52 percent. That's a 50 percent tax increase on everyone.

If they chose to raise taxes just on the top two tax brackets, the rates would jump to 86 percent and 91 percent respectively. At those rates, the affluent would work less and invest less, having a very negative impact on the entire economy. And if you're unlucky enough to be a burner when that's happening, you can kiss a large part of your retirement nest egg—and all of your hard work—goodbye. This is why it's imperative that you work with a knowledgeable and forward-thinking CPA, CFP® practitioner, or tax attorney—in some cases all three—in planning your affairs.

WHAT YOU SHOULD KNOW
ABOUT THE GOVERNMENT'S LIABILITIES

There are four major issues of concern lying in wait like sleeping dragons at the feet of the federal government. These are: social security, health care (including Medicare, Medicaid, and the Affordable Care Act), pensions, and growing annual government spending.

The Social Security Administration estimates that by 2037, the Social Security Trust Fund will be exhausted, and there will only be enough money left to pay about seventy-six cents for every dollar benefit that has been promised.

Health care, particularly as it stretches to accommodate the concerns of our aging population (remember, there are two baby booms at play here—the original Boomers and, eventually, Generation Y), will continue to cost both the government and the average taxpayer more and more money. Recent estimates state that in the future, one out of every five dollars will be spent on health care. This is a scenario where much has been promised, particularly regarding the recently passed Affordable Care Act, but little has been actually funded.

Promised government pension plans, some of which are estimated to be underfunded by trillions of dollars, as well as the ongoing annual spending of our government programs, represent a tremendous future tax burden.

Many people confuse the idea of government stimulus with the government creation of wealth. The simple fact is that, while stimulus packages contribute to the stimulation of the economy, there's a very big—and very real—difference between stimulation and *creation*. The government has no way to create wealth. The only way that they can attain wealth is to tax the ones who do create it—individuals and businesses. And the best bridge programs that the government was ever able to create for itself are the very retirement plans that many investors hope to live on in their golden years: taxable IRAs and 401(k)s.

The theory behind these popular retirement vehicles is that an investor puts money in while working and in a higher tax bracket and then withdraws that money when he retires in a lower tax bracket because, of course, they are no longer earning an income. But the problem is that, in practice, the opposite may very likely occur. In the future, if tax rates increase as projected, we may be withdrawing our money at a higher tax rate than when we actually put it in. Also, keep in mind, often when we retire we have lost many of our deductions—the kids have grown up and moved on, and the house is paid for—so we have little to offset the taxable income coming from our retirement accounts, likely causing us to take money out at a higher tax rate. This seems illogical, and is certainly contrary to the theory used to recommend these investment vehicles.[1]

Fortunately, there are some solutions that the savvy investor and his team can employ in combating these burdensome problems to come.

---

1. Nationally prominent CPA Ed Slott has written extensively about these contradictions in his books *Parlay Your IRA into a Family Fortune* and *The Retirement Savings Time Bomb…and How To Defuse It*. I recommend these books to anyone I come across in the hopes that they will glean from the texts what I did, and help clients avoid needless taxation down the line.

SOLVING THE TAX PROBLEM

One wonderful solution to this quandary is to begin contributing to Roth 401(k)s and Roth IRAs. The amount that you invest is not tax deductible at the time of investment, but the entire amount, growth and all, is income *tax-free*. If you're just starting your investment strategy, or if you're looking to take advantage of a better retention plan in terms of your investments, this is the way to go.

By the same token, if you haven't done so yet, you should utilize the power of Roth conversions. By utilizing your option to convert your traditional IRAs into Roth IRAs, you pay taxes now, in what may be a lower tax bracket, rather than later in life when tax rates may actually be higher. Because there are no longer any income limits on who is eligible to convert their accounts to Roth IRAs, in most cases, this can make a lot of sense.

Of course, there are many factors to consider: how much income you are earning in the conversion year, if you can actually cover and pay taxes on the conversion, and similar considerations. However, in most cases, even with these considerations included, converting your tax-deductible IRAs to Roth IRAs makes a tremendous amount of sense, because the money becomes income tax-free and forever will be—not only for your spouse, but for your children and beyond who may eventually inherit your money.

A third solution may come as a bit of a surprise, but it's perfectly legal, ethical, and doable for most investors. It is possible (and in some cases, advisable) to use life insurance as an effective investment tool. CPA Ed Slott, whom I referred to earlier, has been on record as referring to life insurance as "one of the three biggest benefits of the US tax code that most people miss."

A word of warning before we venture further into the subject—and this is probably why most people are missing this benefit of the US tax code, by the way—proven expertise in this area is required when making a strategy. A poorly designed, poorly funded life insurance policy can be a *bad* investment, much as any investment in the wrong hands can be ineffective at best and detrimental at worst.

In brief, the key to making a life insurance policy work as an investment vehicle for you is to maximize cash value and minimize the death benefit. The IRS sets legal limits on how to do this. The code was adjusted in the 1990s, when tax rates increased on the wealthy and many of these affluent Americans began pouring huge sums of money into tax-free single premium cash value life insurance policies. Staying within the legal limits is the key.

If you have twenty or more years to go until retirement, this may be something you'll want to consider. The main advantage of accumulating cash in a life insurance policy is that, if structured properly, it will never be taxed. The use of withdrawals and loans from the insurance company provide ways to keep this asset tax-free. On the downside, life insurance does have a high cost associated with it, and you may have a lower internal rate of return than you would in, say, a mutual fund or in stocks in the general market. But it's important to note that when you add in the fact that the distributions may not be taxed, you may end up with a higher *net sum* of money than you would with that same mutual fund or stock portfolio. Remember, the cost of the insurance is less than the cost of the taxation. That's worth repeating: the cost of the insurance is less than the cost of the taxation.

Many clients are surprised when they hear me advocate for life insurance, and this is largely due to the fact that, as a product, it's poorly understood and rife with assumptions and potential miscalculations. Life insurance is often oversold—or set up poorly—by the average advisor, but in the case of the top tax attorneys that I work with, it's one of their top planning tools. It's true that if you pay an off-the-shelf premium—meaning you buy a life insurance policy and pay the minimum premium against it so that your family is covered in the event of your death—it's not really an investment vehicle. But if you pay above and beyond the premium, up to the limits that the government sets for contributions, that money earns interest or credits that can be accessed at any time, possibly tax-free.

This is favorable when compared to an IRA or 401(k), which can't be accessed until you are over fifty-nine and a half years of age, and which have limits on how much you can borrow or dictate if you can even gain early access at all. With life insurance, you can access the cash value at any point in time, and do so likely free of tax.

A lot of small business owners, who often tell me that banks will only give them money when they *don't* need it and won't give it to them when they do, turn to life insurance as a funding vehicle for their retirement or business needs, socking away additional cash for the rainy days that are sure to come. Finally, as opposed to 401(k)s and IRAs, the custodians of life insurance policies aren't required to report cash values to the government—meaning you're holding your cards close to your vest.

I always tell my clients, "It's the score at the end of the game that counts." It's not about how much you make, or how much you have at any given moment—it's how much you get to keep. It's the amount of tax-free or after-tax income that really matters—and that's what we, as intelligent investors, should really focus on.

DISINHERITING THE GOVERNMENT

As much as we don't like to think about it, it's not just the amount of after-tax or tax-free income that we have when we're alive that matters, either. For many of us, particularly if we have children or families that we help support, it's important to leave a financial legacy.

For many hardworking people, these issues start to come up six months after we turn seventy and a half. At that point, according to current tax law, the government forces those individuals to take money out of their 401(k)s and IRAs. These are called *required minimum distributions*, and they must be taken even if the investor doesn't need the money. Many of my clients find these to be a nuisance, and an uncomfortable tax burden. Those same clients often ask me what they should do with the money after they've withdrawn it, noting that the purpose of their investments has always been to function as a nest egg for their children or family when they are no longer around.

These clients are surprised when I tell them that the 401(k) or IRA is one of the *worst* assets for their children to inherit, owing to the amount of taxes that will be taken from it. IRAs and 401(k)s not only are subject to income taxation, but to potentially parallel estate taxes as well. If you have a large enough estate and large enough IRA/401(k) investments, you could lose 75 to 85 percent of the value to taxes upon your death, leaving less of an inheritance than you originally intended.

Much as the life insurance product represents one potential out-of-the-box solution for wealth accumulation, there's another equally effective strategy for disinheriting the tax man that's equally legal and ethically sound. It all stems from beneficiary planning—which, again, requires some forethought and the proper guidance.

Let's use the hypothetical situation of Bob and Mary, a married couple with two children, Suzy and John. Bob's primary retirement and inheritance vehicle is an IRA worth $1 million. He's named his wife, Mary, as the primary beneficiary of this IRA, and his two children are equally named as secondary beneficiaries, splitting it fifty-fifty. This strategy is straightforward enough, but there's a significant problem with it: taxes.

After Bob passes on, Mary inherits the IRA tax-free, thanks to the unlimited marital deduction. She receives sound investment advice for the remainder of her lifetime, and the IRA eventually grows from Bob's original $1 million to $2 million. The average woman in America, incidentally, outlives her husband by about fifteen years, so this scenario is far from outlandish. However, once her children inherit the IRA after she dies a few years later, the value of their inheritance takes a massive tax hit that may wipe out nearly half of the IRA, depending on tax rates at that time and size of the rest of their estate. The tax man becomes the biggest single beneficiary.

With the proper planning, this scenario could have turned out differently. By utilizing a properly structured life insurance policy in addition to the IRA, it's possible for Bob and Mary to leave a financial legacy that survives them much more intact than just relying on their children directly inheriting the money as the secondary beneficiaries. In this scenario, Bob still names Mary as the primary beneficiary on the IRA, and they both enjoy full control of the money in their lifetimes. But now, instead of naming the children as secondary beneficiaries, they name a qualified charity: their church, their former college, a scholarship fund for needy children, or an environmental group, for example. In this case, the IRS cannot tax the money from the IRA that goes to that charity, and Bob and Mary have been able to pay it forward, leaving a legacy to the community that they lived in and to a cause they care about.

If you're worried that I've forgotten about their two children, don't worry, we're getting to that part. This is where the properly structured life insurance policy comes in. Because many people don't need the required minimum distributions of their IRA for day-to-day living expenses—particularly people at the level of wealth that Bob and Mary had reached—those proceeds can be spent elsewhere. If those required minimum distributions are used to buy life insurance, those death benefit proceeds pass income tax-free—and possibly estate tax-free—into the hands of the beneficiaries.

So, in this scenario, Bob and Mary have full access to the money throughout their lifetimes, their remaining IRA funds are put to great social use when donated tax-free to charity, and their children inherit a check, entirely tax-free, from the life insurance company. Everybody wins. Except, of course, the tax man.

You don't have to be spectacularly wealthy to benefit from this strategy, either; you simply need to have an efficient plan in place in distributing your assets to your children. I've seen multimillionaire clients do this and I've helped clients with only a couple hundred thousand in their IRAs do the same.

A NOTE ABOUT ESTATE TAX EXEMPTIONS AND STRETCH IRAS

Apart from the strategies described above, there are two other items that merit mentioning. Although you could easily write a book on each of the subjects on their own, it's not something that I'll be going too deeply into, although I'm always happy to entertain any further questions you might have, as will any reputable tax advisor or financial planner.

Much like life insurance, proper estate tax planning often suffers from certain preconceptions in the public domain. People seem to think that it's only for the wealthy, and that anyone who isn't worth millions shouldn't worry about it. This is far from the case. Estate planning isn't only for the wealthy—it's for everyone. A married couple is granted an exemption for each spouse, and this can be very large. As of this writing, a married couple can deduct $10.5 *million* from their estate and pass it to their heirs.

Just because the ceiling is spectacularly high doesn't mean you should be intimidated if you aren't anywhere near it—so much the better for your estate planning purposes. You simply can't afford *not* to consider this valuable exemption, particularly if you are on the wealthier side. Recently deceased actor James Gandolfini is a prime example: when he passed away unexpectedly last year, he had no estate plan at all—and a large part of his net worth is now going to the federal government.

While many clients rely on these exemptions to pass large amounts of their estate to their heirs tax-free, there are reasons to begin to use the exemption well before a client dies. There's leverage to be had in a proper estate tax exemption strategy. By simply notifying the IRS through the proper channels (i.e., filing a gift tax return) you can begin gifting portions of your estate now—up to that total lifetime exemption amount—to your heirs tax-free.

I often see this in situations where family-owned businesses are beginning to transition from one generation to the next, or if land is about to escalate in value due to development or exploration. Gifting an asset now before it appreciates allows that future appreciation to be realized after the transfer (a warning here: this can be tricky and requires proper tax and legal counsel). Furthermore, these gifts can be used to purchase life insurance, much like I advised the hypothetical couple seeking to make the most out of the required minimum distributions from their IRA. Can you imagine how much life insurance a $10.5 million premium could buy, depending on age and health? The answer is $25 million, or $50 million, or maybe $100 million, and if held in an irrevocable life insurance trust (ILIT), it's all tax-free. Now *that's* leverage.

A recent example of this was reported by the *San Jose Mercury News* when they ran a story about an unnamed Silicon Valley billionaire who purchased the world's largest known amount of life insurance: $201 million of coverage. Now that's someone who truly understands leverage.

The last often-overlooked benefit of the tax code, again according to Ed Slott, is what we call the stretch IRA. Using this is simply a matter of educating the beneficiaries, and is another excellent example of how knowledge truly is power. When a beneficiary inherits an IRA from his parents, he has three primary options: accepting a lump sum payment, which is taxed all at once; accepting a five-year payout, in which he can spread distributions (and the resultant taxes) out over five years; or spreading the distributions out over his lifetime by using the required minimum distributions calculated for his younger age.

Unfortunately, many people choose to take the lump sum in this situation. This is an example of where patience would be a virtue—if the heir were to spread the required minimum distributions out over his lifetime, most of the money would stay *inside* the IRA, and thus remain free of taxes until needed and withdrawn. This allows for the IRA to continue growing, creating a much larger legacy. Beneficiary education is one of the benefits you get from working with a qualified advisor.

As I've noted several times within this chapter—and it bears repeating once more—all of this can be complicated, and all of it requires good counsel. It's imperative that you work with experienced and knowledgeable tax and finance professionals and/or a highly qualified estate tax attorney. Their knowledge can be *your* power—and ultimately, your financial legacy.

CHAPTER SEVEN

You Can't Do It Alone—
Finding a Financial Advisor

Investing can be a confusing prospect, one that is further muddled by emotional factors, as I've talked about in previous chapters. If there's one lesson that I've learned over time in this business, it's that individual investors—no matter how well intentioned or savvy—should not serve as their own investment advisors. In legal circles, "The man who represents himself has a fool for a client," is a popular way of expressing this sentiment. The same is true in investing.

Simply put: you can't do it alone. It's not a failure to admit this; it's wisdom. Having a financial advisor means that you've got someone in your corner who can take a truly objective, well-researched look at your priorities and goals and help you achieve those priorities and goals by protecting and growing your assets. In fact, in a recent Vanguard Funds study titled "Putting Value on Your Value," it was determined that Vanguard investors who used a financial advisor received around 3 percent more per year in returns as compared to those investors who did it themselves.

According to that study, financial advisors offered the following value points:

1. Being an effective behavioral coach
2. Applying an asset location strategy
3. Employing cost-effective investments
4. Maintaining the proper allocation through rebalancing
5. Implementing a spending strategy

But there's more to the process of choosing a financial advisor than just finding one. It's very surprising to me how many people fail to vet the person they're working with, either because they haven't thought to or they simply don't know how to. And in thirty years in the business, I've run across some absolute horror stories stemming from the failure of clients to properly research their financial advisor. If you were going to have heart surgery, you would probably Google your surgeon—or the hospital, at the very least—to find out if there have been any complaints about that hospital or the surgeon. If you were giving your money to charity, you would probably look on a website such as Charity Navigator to make sure that the charity in question actually exists and actually does the good work it claims to do.

So why is it that when confronted with the prospect of finding a financial advisor, so many people take these so-called advisors at their word when trusting them with their most precious assets, their most private information, and their very futures? I don't have the answer to that question, unfortunately, but I do have some advice for your consideration, and it all revolves around arming yourself with the most powerful weapon at any investor's disposal: knowledge.

The first thing to understand about the investment industry is that the terms *financial advisor* and *investment advisor* don't actually mean anything. You can call yourself a financial advisor and it's no different than being the head dishwasher at a restaurant. Being a financial advisor is not a credential, nor is it a term that confers any designation. Furthermore, if the words *financial advisor* or *investment advisor* are the only ones under the advisor's name on his business card, it's probably a sign that he's not particularly dedicated to his profession.

In this profession, you continue to learn, or you fall behind. You take opportunities to pursue continuing education, earning credentials and designations that signal you're up on the best practices of the industry. Credentials such as CFP® certification, ChFC®, and CLU mean that the professionals bearing those designations have been tested and vetted by outside entities. They take time and expertise to achieve. So looking for these additional designations and credentials is a good first step.

But it's not enough to stop there. Dishonest people will forever be finding new ways to be dishonest. Thankfully, there exist ways to verify the credentials and history of the professional you're considering trusting with your money. Much like a surgeon with a history of malpractice complaints can't step into a time machine and reverse them or cover up the paper trail, a financial professional with a history of complaints, sanctions, and termination events can't cover those up, either. And while it's possible to say that you have a credential that you do not possess, it's harder to get away with it, particularly in this Internet age.

By Googling your candidates, at the very minimum, you'll easily be able to find a wealth of information. Checking with the Better Business Bureau (www.bbb.org) is another essential step. If the professional is insurance licensed, check with the state insurance commission and find out if there have been any violations on his or her record. If the representative has a securities license, they'll also be listed by the Financial Industry Regulatory Authority (www.finra.org/brokercheck), where it's easy to pull up a detailed history on them, including complaints and settlements, in mere minutes.

On FINRA's site, you can also view their employment history; this is useful because if a professional has changed broker/dealers frequently, it may be a red flag. You can also check on the quality of those broker/dealers listed as well, making sure that they're reputable operations with a large enough scale to stay in business or have the resources to settle any disputes that may arise. While a vast majority of professionals are honest and reputable, there are still some that aren't. You don't have to look very far to come up with examples of these types of people, particularly if you've been in the business as long as I have.

I recall looking into one so-called financial advisor for a client and discovering that the advisor had had so many regulatory problems that he actually *changed his name* in order to operate under the radar. Ultimately, he lost his securities license, but that didn't stop him—he still had a state insurance license and was sticking his clients into annuities that benefited him first and foremost. When the regulatory bodies caught up to him, they found that although he was living in a palatial estate where he met with his clients and drove a fleet of brand-new cars, he didn't own a fraction of it. He was leasing the cars. He was renting the house.

Don't take any chances when it comes to your money.

Just as financial advisor isn't really a designation, so is the similar-sounding investment advisor. There are no actual professional certifications or designations implied in this title. Many professionals who have this written on their business cards are, in fact, insurance agents masquerading as investment professionals—they don't even have a securities license!

The bottom line here is not to be satisfied when you hear that the rep you're working with calls him or herself a financial advisor or investment advisor. You have to do a little digging to figure out exactly what their qualifications are, and exactly who has their back while they're watching yours.

Size is critical here; it's expensive to run a broker/dealer, or a Registered Investment Advisory (RIA), and so you should make sure they have the critical mass to do proper oversight of their reps and have the financial strength to handle any liabilities that may come their way. Another important area that can't be overlooked is which custodian is in custody of your money. Charles Schwab, NFS (National Financial Services), and Pershing are examples of a few of the nationally recognizable custodians—they're the ones who do all of the reporting, and the ones who hold or take custody of the assets and create the documentation generated by each trade and transaction.

You also have to make sure that the broker/dealer and investment advisor you're working with aren't one and the same. In other words, some people establish their own broker/dealerships and take custody of the accounts that they clear their transactions through—essentially removing any checks and balances of the traditional IAR/broker/dealer relationship.

Bernie Madoff is the most classic and recently recognizable example of this. Because he was his own custodian and broker/dealer, there was a lack of regulation where there normally should have been ample regulation. If the broker/dealer and investment advisor are one and the same, then there's effectively less oversight. There's none of the third-party reporting that goes on with a reputable broker/dealer and custodian, and it's extremely easy to fudge the truth in those circumstances.

In my own situation, I clear through a nationally prominent broker/dealer, but I own my own practice. Which means that I have my own personal financial net worth very much tied to my ability to serve my own clients, and to grow and operate in a fair and respectable manner. My *family's* financial well-being is tied to the well-being of my clients and the success of my firm, which means I've got some skin in the game.

While it's obviously possible to get good advice and service from a national firm, there's something to be said for the independently owned enterprise. I have a greater appreciation of the value of a client because I do not have the national branding of a Merrill Lynch, or, say, a Wells Fargo, nor do I have a constant stream of clients being fed to me by a large bank or local credit union. When I develop a new client relationship, I intend on having that relationship for life.

These are just a few examples of the red flags that I've seen pop up over the years of working with clients who have come to me after being burned—or worrying that they were about to be burned. It even goes for those who are vice presidents of investments or accounts at large firms; again, that isn't a professional designation. All that this means is that they've been successful at growing the business for their bank or brokerage firm; they've moved from the bull pen to the corner office.

So what credentials *should* you look for?

First, the toughest credential to earn is probably the Chartered Financial Analyst, or CFA. You don't typically see this designation in the retail community. Usually, CFAs are someone working as the money manager or research analyst of a big mutual fund or for a big investment advisor. It requires several years of work experience, extensive testing, and extensive continuing education credits. This is a tough and rigorous designation to get, and one that undoubtedly commands respect.

A high standard that *any* investment client should look for is Certified Financial Planner (CFP®). This designation requires several years of experience, extensive coursework, and testing. It takes a large amount of continuing education to maintain this designation, meaning that if you've found a verified CFP® professional, you've found someone who takes learning about their industry seriously. CFP® professionals pride themselves on having a very high professional standard, and are well respected not only within the financial industry, but also by the attorneys, tax professionals, and estate planners who often work with them.

On the insurance side, you'll also see the designations CLU and ChFC®—Chartered Life Underwriter and Chartered Financial Consultant. Obtained through the American College in Bryn Mawr, Pennsylvania, these professionals have to undergo coursework, continuing education, and testing to maintain these designations as well.

Ultimately, the most important tool in making sure you're well taken care of—other than the research methods I've outlined above—might be common sense. You would be well advised to remember that all investment professionals are essentially fishing out of the same pond. If someone claims to have a perfect strategy that absolutely can't lose, or that they have developed a strategy that perfectly times the market, that should make you suspicious. The perfect strategy doesn't exist.

What these claims do mean is that if something sounds too good to be true, bottom line, it's too good to be true. There's no scientific way to ensure the consistent repeatability of performance. A good, honest financial advisor will not tell you that they'll always beat the market, or that you won't have time periods where your investment returns will disappoint. Instead, what a good financial advisor will give you is real returns that will be better if you work with them as compared to not working with them. A good financial advisor can keep you on track, helping prevent you from making irrational emotional decisions that will destroy your long-term planning.

There are no superstar managers who always outperform, and no bulletproof strategies. But there are good people out there, and I'm confident that you can find them. I would love to be the person to help you.

CHAPTER 8

A Community Call to Action

Ultimately, I like to think that I got into this business not just because it was my calling to help others with their financial bottom line, but because I get the opportunity to help them make their dreams and goals reality. As I shared early on in the book, my story is part of what makes me unique: I'm a self-made man, and I know the irreplaceable value of hard work and the fighting spirit.

But the other thing that makes me unique as a financial professional is that, in building my own firm, I've achieved independence. And that means that not only do I own my book of business, unlike the stockbrokers and advisors who work for big-name firms, but also that my well-being—and my family's well-being—is tied in with the success of my clients.

The other day, I was sitting in my family room contemplating a simple plaque we have hanging over our fireplace that says "Live, Laugh, Love." I translated those words a bit further into a deeper meaning in my own life: live large, laugh often, and love always.

Living large isn't about driving a Ferrari or living in a country club neighborhood. It's participating in life. Giving people something of generosity. Making the lives of people around you better. That's living large. Laughing often is no problem for me; I'm a real practical joker, and I think it's important to laugh at yourself and at life.

And I've already seen the last one come true. I always lead with a loving heart in my life, and the love has come back to me. And that's what I'm hoping to do here, when all is said and done.

Because of my prioritizing people over portfolios, I've always looked for ways to pay my fortunes forward. I think it's not just good business sense, but essential human obligation to leave this world a better place than we found it. That spirit was alive in my mother and father, and I want to keep it living on in me. Through my practice, much of this paying it forward has involved working on financial matters with integrity and purpose, helping my clients along the way. But I've started a new endeavor recently, one I truly believe in, and I'm hoping you'll join me in taking advantage of what it has to offer.

No matter what your station in life, what your career, what your family situation or your financial situation, you're probably less organized than you need to be. That's not a judgment on anyone personally, it's just a fact. I'm lumping myself in there, too. It's hard to think about these uncomfortable inevitabilities—the fact that something awful might happen, or that time might just take its time, leaving family members in the lurch as they struggle to grieve and move on. Nothing breaks my heart more than knowing that people are suffering financial and legal pain while they're already suffering the emotional pain of loss.

I've seen this firsthand, in my life and in the lives of my clients. I've had clients tell me stories about traumatic events. One client told me about how his wife had a seizure and was incapacitated and taken to the hospital. When he joined her there after the ambulance ride, he was panic- and grief-stricken, and had to fill out mountains of paperwork regarding insurance and health history and care directives and the like. He had absolutely no idea what medication his wife was taking, or where they'd placed their durable medical powers of attorney and living will. Some of it was no doubt lost in the heat of the moment, but the bigger issue remains: if we don't know where things are and what to look for when it's not a crisis, the situation is only going to be further complicated and confusing when it *is* hitting crisis levels.

We're often too busy to organize our lives, but it's also the truth that we simply don't believe that anything bad is going to happen to us. It's human nature to think we're indestructible. And we're a society that moves fast, throwing paperwork in different drawers in different locations, saving things to take care of later, not finalizing important documents such as living wills and durable powers of attorney, just because we always think we're going to have another day, another week, another month to do it.

But if you lose someone suddenly, you also realize that even if you have all of these documents done and your life insurance plans in order, it still can take forever to locate everything. My lawyer friends are always telling me that client execution or lack thereof causes more boondoggles or delays in executing a well thought out estate plan. Assets are not always titled properly to take advantage of the estate plan, leaving an unnecessary mess behind.

As you can see, I feel very passionate about this subject. My experiences, and the experiences of my parents and their parents before them, have all influenced how I live my life. When I say I'm trying to pay it forward, I have a beautifully simple, entirely free proposition for you: I'll help you make the uncomfortable process of this organization safe, efficient, and foolproof.

When I enter into a client relationship, I provide a fire- and waterproof safe and the organizational files to go along with them. In those files, every part of that client's life is compartmentalized. We have files for medical information, financial information, investments, life insurance, credit cards, club memberships, and estate planning documents. You name it, it's in there. When it's all organized, my business card goes right on top of the safe, so if something happens to the client who owns that safe, the person left to pick up the pieces can start to do that easily and with my assistance.

As a husband and father, I know how important it is to have these arrangements set up. Because of my own life experiences, both personally and professionally, I know how life can change in a blink of an eye. I want to be the person who is there for your family.

It would be an honor if you let me start with you.

Acknowledgements

For years I have contemplated writing this book. I have felt my story is pretty unique, and very much an American success story.

Through my formative years I was lucky to have been blessed with great friends from great families who themselves have all become very successful. I think it was a blessing to have been raised in a small town in Iowa where honesty and hard work are the norms. I was always taught that hard work was a blessing from God.

Learning to work at a young age, I developed my work ethic early in life. I had my first job when I was ten. I made sixty cents an hour cleaning the local drive-in at six in the morning. By age twelve I was pouring concrete during the day for two dollars an hour and playing baseball at night. I had a summer job pouring concrete until I finished college.

During my years at the University of South Dakota, I had the opportunity to develop great friendships that still last today. Many of the friends I met in college are some of the most successful and solid people I have had the pleasure to meet.

I have had the great pleasure of marrying my best friend, and God has blessed us with three beautiful children. Through the years of raising our children we have developed many close friends as our kids have gone through school and pursued their athletic interests. I have had the great pleasure of seeing my kids win five state championships, four in basketball and one in football. There was even one night a few years back where my son Christian and daughter, Carsen, won state championships in basketball on the same night in back-to-back games.

I have had the opportunity to share a business partnership with some of the most honest and ethical financial advisors that exist in the industry. I have been blessed to develop friendships and working relationships with courageous and loving people I proudly call clients. When reading this book, I hope you feel the love and passion with which I try and live my life.

Thank you and I look forward to helping you soon.

For more information contact:
Kurt D. Cambier
303-271-1067
kcambier@cambridgeresource.com

CPSIA information can be obtained
at www.ICGtesting.com
Printed in the USA
LVOW10*0334281216
518873LV00003B/4/P